cooking the Greek way

Sweets such as *melópitta (left)* and *toúrta mé portokáli ké yaoúrti* are often served with tiny cups of thick Greek coffee. (Recipes on pages 44 and 42.)

cooking the
Greek way

LYNNE W. VILLIOS

PHOTOGRAPHS BY ROBERT L. & DIANE WOLFE

easy menu
ethnic
cookbooks

Lerner Publications Company ▪ Minneapolis

Editor: Laura Storms
Drawings and Map by Jeanette Swofford

The page border for this book is based on the Greek key or fret
pattern, known also as a *meander*. This pattern originated around
1000 B.C. and became an often-used motif in classical Greek art.
The term meander comes from the River Meander in Asia Minor
because of that river's winding course.

Library of Congress Cataloging in Publication Data

Villios, Lynne W.
  Cooking the Greek way.

  (Easy menu ethnic cookbooks)
  Includes index.
  Summary: Recipes for authentic Greek foods such as
dolmades, baklava, and spinach pie, plus several other
recipes for main dishes, appetizers, and desserts.
  1. Cookery, Greek—Juvenile literature. [1. Cookery,
Greek] I. Wolfe, Robert L., ill. II. Wolfe, Diane, ill.
III. Swofford, Jeanette, ill. IV. Title. V. Series.
TX723.5.G8V55 1984   641.59495   84-12585
ISBN 0-8225-0910-5 (lib. bdg.)

Manufactured in the United States of America
6 7 8 9 10 11 – P/JR – 02 01 00 99 98 97

**Olives and feta cheese give Greek salad its unique
flavor. (Recipe on page 23.)**

CONTENTS

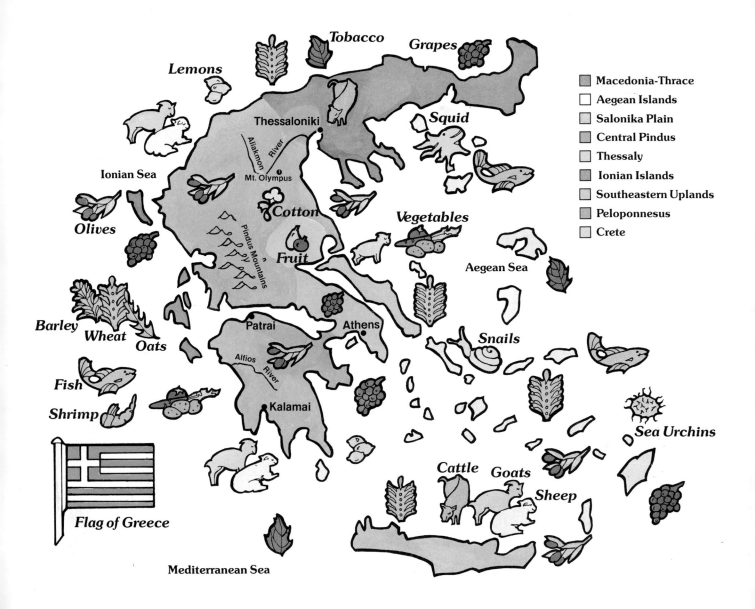

Tobacco

Grapes

Lemons

Squid

Thessaloniki

Aliakmon River

Mt. Olympus

Ionian Sea

Cotton

Vegetables

Olives

Fruit

Aegean Sea

Pindus Mountains

Barley

Wheat

Oats

Patrai

Athens

Snails

Alfios River

Fish

Shrimp

Kalamai

Sea Urchins

Cattle   Goats

Sheep

Flag of Greece

Mediterranean Sea

Macedonia-Thrace
Aegean Islands
Salonika Plain
Central Pindus
Thessaly
Ionian Islands
Southeastern Uplands
Peloponnesus
Crete

INTRODUCTION

When one thinks of Greece, what often comes to mind is the ancient civilization that flourished there thousands of years ago. Ruins of this ancient culture still stand as reminders of Greece's glorious past. Today, Greece is an interesting combination of old and new. Even modern Greek cooking reflects ancient times, with dishes such as *dolmades,* or stuffed grape leaves, dating back thousands of years.

Greek cooking also combines both western European and Middle Eastern influences. (Greece is located between these two regions.) When the Romans invaded Greece in 197 B.C., for instance, they brought with them pasta and tomato sauces. Yogurt, rice, and many pastries came from the Persians, and coffee came from the Turks. These influences, along with those ingredients and methods that are uniquely Greek, created a cuisine that is both rich in tradition and extremely varied.

THE LAND

Greece is a land of sun and sea located in southeastern Europe. The country is surrounded on three sides by the sea: the Ionian Sea to the west, the Mediterranean Sea to the south, and the Aegean Sea to the east. A relatively small country, nearly one-quarter of Greece is made up of islands—437 in all—and can be divided into nine major land regions.

Macedonia-Thrace is a rocky, sparsely populated area in northeastern Greece where tobacco is grown in the many valleys, and other crops are grown in the plains along the coast.

The *Salonika Plain* is Greece's most important agricultural area. Here, fruits, grains, and cotton are grown, and goats, sheep, and other livestock are raised.

Sheep and goats graze in the *Central Pindus* region, a mountainous area where cotton, lemons, and olives are produced.

Thessaly is often called Greece's breadbasket because wheat is grown in abundance there. Fruits and olives are grown in Thessaly as well.

Greek fishermen haul in the day's catch. Fishing is one of Greece's major industries, so fish and seafood dishes are very popular.

Athens, the capital of Greece, is located in the *Southeastern Uplands*. Goats, wheat, and grapes are the major products of this area.

The *Peloponnesus* is a mountainous, rugged peninsula. Only about one-fourth of the land is used for growing crops, but some vegetables, grapes, olives, and grains are grown there. This area is most famous for its ancient ruins.

The *Ionian Islands* in the Ionian Sea produce many crops, including grains, olives, and grapes. Tobacco, grapes, barley, and wheat are the chief products of the *Aegean Islands,* and *Crete,* the largest Greek island, produces olives, grapes, sheep, and beef cattle.

THE FOOD

Greece's climate and geography have always been major influences on its cuisine. The juicy lemons, tangy olives, fresh herbs, and vegetables that grow in Greece's warm sunshine are some of the country's best-loved foods.

Fishing is a major industry in Greece. The Mediterranean, Aegean, and Ionian seas yield bountiful catches, and the Greeks enjoy many fish and seafood dishes, often flavored with oregano—the most popular Greek herb—and fresh lemon juice.

Greece's rocky, barren mountains are ideal for herds of goats and sheep, and these animals provide several important Greek foods. Goat's milk is used both as a beverage and for making cheese, including tangy, white *feta* cheese, the best-known of all Greek cheeses. This salty, crumbly cheese is eaten plain, used in salads, and added to stews and soups. Lamb is the most popular meat in Greece, though chicken, pork, and beef are enjoyed as well. Meats are often grilled over hot coals in outdoor pits. Olive trees grow all over in Greece, and the oil that is pressed from these olives is some of the finest in the world. In Greece, olive oil is used for frying, dressing salads, flavoring foods, and even for making pastry dough. Greeks snack on olives and put them in salads.

Honey, which is found wild in all parts of Greece, is the Greeks' favorite sweetener and is often used in the many very sweet pastries they enjoy. Mount Hymettus near Athens is famous the world over for the wild honey found there.

GREEK COOKING IN ANCIENT TIMES

The art of cooking was appreciated thousands of years ago in ancient Greece. In fact, the world's first cookbook is said to have been written in 350 B.C. by the philosopher Archestratus. At that time, cooks were very highly regarded. They were not thought of as household help but as artists, and they were eagerly sought by employers.

The *"Deipnosophistae,"* or "Philosophy of Dining," was written around A.D. 200 by a Greek man named Athenaeus. It presents a picture of the foods and eating customs of the ancient Greeks, including such famous authors as Sophocles and Homer. According to Athenaeus, the ancient Greeks were the first to eat oysters, to grow cabbage and artichokes, and to create baked goods such as pastries and gingerbread.

The Greeks liked eating food that was very, very hot. In order not to burn their hands and fingers (spoons and forks were not yet invented), they "trained" themselves to withstand the hot temperatures by dipping their hands into hotter and hotter liquids every day.

Napkins were not invented until the 15th century, so the clothes of the ancient Greeks got very dirty at mealtime. Polite diners changed clothes between courses in order to appear clean and tidy.

The ancient Greeks had some other customs and beliefs that we consider odd today. Grasshoppers were one of their greatest delicacies. They often served lettuce soup at the end of an evening meal because they thought it helped them sleep. Ancient Greeks also believed that honey could make them live longer. Democritus, a Greek who lived to be 109 years old, said the secret to his long life was eating honey and rubbing his skin with olive oil!

S. A. Johnson

The Temple of Hephaestus in Athens *(above)* **is the best-preserved of Greece's many ancient temples.**

THE PEOPLE AND THEIR CUSTOMS

Today family ties and traditions are very important to the Greeks. The whole family comes together for the evening meal, which is usually eaten at about 10 P.M. Everyday family dinners are generally very simple. On holidays, however, it is traditional to have much more elaborate meals.

Nearly all Greeks belong to the Greek Orthodox Church, and most Greek holidays are religious in nature. Traditional foods are served on these special days. At Easter, the most important Greek holiday, lamb flavored with herbs and roasted over hot coals is served. Braided bread decorated with red-dyed eggs is a traditional Easter food as well. One Greek Easter custom is for each member of the family to hold an egg in the palm of his or her hand and to crack the egg against one held by someone else. The person whose egg breaks first is the "winner." The deep-red eggs symbolize the blood of Christ, and the cracking of the eggs symbolizes the Resurrection.

At Christmas, roast suckling pig, special holiday breads, and butter cookies are traditional foods. New Year's Day is a very special holiday. It is also known as the Feast of St. Basil, the saint who answers wishes and brings gifts. On the Feast of St. Basil, the Greeks serve a special cake in which a silver coin is baked. Tradition says that whoever receives the piece of cake containing the coin will have good luck for the coming year. Another New Year's Day custom involves breaking open a pomegranate on the doorstep of the home. If the fruit has many seeds, the year will be a happy and prosperous one for the family.

The Greeks are known for their hospitality and love of entertaining. A Greek would never think not to offer a visitor something to eat or drink, and it would be considered just as rude for a visitor to refuse the offer. One tradition is to offer a guest a *glyko*, or "spoon sweet," which is a thick jam of fruits or vegetables such as peach, quince, apricot, tomato, or eggplant. The *glyko* is served on a tray with a glass of ice water and a cup of thick, sweet Greek coffee. Offering these treats welcomes the visitor and shows the family's happiness at having a guest.

With the following recipes, you can prepare authentic and delicious Greek meals for your own family and friends. Make the meal a festive occasion, as the Greeks do, by enjoying lively conversation along with the flavorful foods. As the Greeks would say, "Kalí orexí!" (Happy eating!)

BEFORE YOU BEGIN

Cooking any dish, plain or fancy, is easier and more fun if you are familiar with its ingredients. Greek cooking makes use of some ingredients that you may not know. You should also be familiar with the special terms that will be used in various recipes in this book. Therefore, *before* you start cooking any of the Greek dishes in this book, study the following "dictionary" of special ingredients and terms very carefully. Then read through the recipe you want to try from beginning to end.

Now you are ready to shop for ingredients and to organize the cookware you will need. Once you have assembled everything, you can begin to cook. It is also very important to read *The Careful Cook* on page 47 before you start. Following these rules will make your cooking experience safe, fun, and easy.

COOKING UTENSILS

colander — A bowl-shaped dish with holes in it that is used for washing or draining food

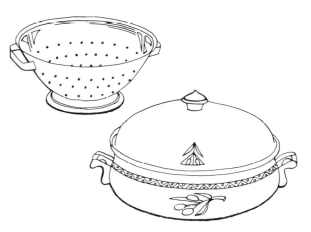

dutch oven — A heavy pot with a tight-fitting domed cover that is often used for cooking soups or stews

pastry brush — A small brush with nylon bristles used for coating food with melted butter or other liquids

skewer — A thin metal rod used to hold small pieces of meat or vegetables for broiling

spatula — A flat, thin utensil, usually metal, used to lift, toss, turn, or scoop up food

whisk — A small wire utensil used for beating foods by hand

COOKING TERMS

baste—To pour, brush, or spoon liquid over food as it roasts in order to flavor and moisten it

boil—To heat a liquid over high heat until bubbles form and rise rapidly to the surface

broil—To cook directly under a heat source so that the side of the food facing the heat cooks rapidly

brown—To cook food quickly in fat over high heat so that the surface turns an even brown

dash—a small amount; a quick shake or sprinkle

fold—To blend an ingredient with other ingredients by using a gentle overturning circular motion instead of by stirring or beating

garnish—To decorate with a small piece of food such as parsley

grate—To cut into tiny pieces by rubbing the food against a grater

marinate—To soak food in a liquid in order to add flavor and to tenderize it

mince—To chop food into very small pieces

preheat—To allow an oven to warm up to a certain temperature before putting food in it

roast—To cook in an open pan in an oven so that heat penetrates the food from all sides

sauté—To fry quickly over high heat in oil or fat, stirring or turning the food to prevent burning

simmer—To cook over low heat in liquid kept just below its boiling point. Bubbles may occasionally rise to the surface.

Garlic and onions are often sautéed before they are added to other ingredients in a recipe. Here sautéed garlic and onions are lifted out of the pan with a spatula.

SPECIAL INGREDIENTS

almond extract—A liquid made from the oil of the almond nut and used to give an almond flavor to food

bay leaf—The dried leaf of the bay (also called laurel) tree. It is used to season food.

currants—Small, dried, seedless grapes similar to raisins

dill—An herb whose seeds and leaves are both used in cooking. Dried dill is called *dill weed.*

feta cheese—A crumbly, white cheese made from goat's milk

grape leaves—The leaves of grape-vine plants, usually found packed in jars with brine (salt water) and used in many Greek recipes as wrappers for various fillings

Greek olives—Black olives, usually pickled in brine (salt water), with wrinkled skin and a slightly tart taste

lentils—Brown, flat, dried beans

marjoram—A fragrant herb of the mint family often used in Greek cooking

olive oil—An oil made by pressing olives. It is used in cooking and for dressing salads

orzo—A small, rice-shaped pasta

phyllo—Paper-thin dough used in many Greek recipes. Phyllo is available frozen at many supermarkets and at specialty stores.

pine nuts—The edible seed of certain pine trees. Pine nuts are rather expensive; chopped almonds or walnuts are good substitutes.

red-wine vinegar—A vinegar made with red wine that is often used with oil for dressing salads

ricotta cheese—A white cheese made with whole or skim milk that resembles cottage cheese

scallions—A variety of green onion

slivered almonds—Almonds that have been split into thin strips

A GREEK MENU

Below is a simplified menu plan for a typical day of Greek cooking. The Greek names of the dishes are given, along with a guide on how to pronounce them. Two alternate lunch and three dinner ideas are included.

ENGLISH	GREEK	PRONUNCIATION GUIDE
Breakfast	*Próyefma*	PRO-yev-mah
Lunch	*Yéfma*	YEV-mah
I	I	
Skewered Lamb	Arní Souvlákia	Ahr-NEE soov-LAH-khee-ah
Greek Salad	Saláta	sah-LAH-tah
Rice Pudding	Rizógalo	ree-ZOH-ghah-loh
II	II	
Spinach Pie	Spanikópita	spah-nee-KOH-pee-tah
Greek Salad	Saláta	sah-LAH-tah
Fruit and Yogurt	Fróuta ké Yaoúrtí	FROO-tah keh ee-ah-OOR-tee
Butter Cookies	Kourabiéthes	koo-rah-BEETH-ehs
Appetizers	*Mezéthes*	meh-ZETH-ehs
Eggplant Salad	Melitzánosaláta	meh-leet-ZAH-noh-sah-LAH-tah
Cucumber and Yogurt Dip	Tzatzíki	dzah-DZEE-kee
Lentil Soup	Fakí	fah-KEH
Stuffed Grape Leaves	Dolmádes	dole-MAHD-ehs
Egg and Lemon Soup	Soúpa Avgolémono	SOO-pah av-ghoh-LEH-mo-noh

ENGLISH	GREEK	PRONUNCIATION GUIDE
Dinner	**Déipnon**	DEEP-noh
I	I	
Beef and Onion Stew	Stifádo	stee-FAH-doh
Rice Pilaf	Piláfi	pee-LAH-fee
Fried Zucchini	Kolokithákia Tiganíta	ko-lo-kee-THAH-kee-ah tee-gahn-EE-tah
Greek Salad	Saláta	sah-LAH-tah
Honey Cheese Pie	Melópitta	meh-LOH-pee-tah
II	II	
Baked Fish	Psári Plakí	PSAH-ree plah-KEE
Baked Potatoes Oregano	Patátes Foúrno Riganátes	pah-TAH-tehs FOOR-noh ree-gah-NAH-tehs
Stuffed Tomatoes with Feta Cheese	Domátes mé Féta	doh-MAH-tehs meh FEH-tah
Orange Yogurt Cake	Toúrta mé Portokáli ké Yaoúrtí	TOOR-tah meh por-toh-KAH lee keh ee-ah-OOR-tee
III	III	
Roast Chicken	Kótapoulo Foúrnou	KO-tah-poo-loh FOOR-noh
Orzo with Browned Butter Sauce	Órzo Kaúto Voútyro	OR-zoh KAU-to VOO-tee-roh
Greek Salad	Saláta	sah-LAH-tah
Walnut-Honey Pastry	Baklavá	bah-klah-VAH

BREAKFAST/ Próyefma

The Greek people generally do not eat a large breakfast. They begin their day with a simple meal of fresh fruit, cheese, bread, and thick, strong coffee. In small Greek towns and villages, bread dough is often mixed and shaped in the morning at home and then taken to the local baker who bakes everyone's loaves in a communal oven. (Many rural Greeks do not have their own ovens.) The Greeks are very fond of breads, especially sweet yeast breads, and form them into special traditional shapes for holidays.

LUNCH/ Yéfma

In Greece, the midday meal is often eaten at around 1:00 or 2:00. In the cities, lunch is a rather light meal, much like lunch in the United States. In rural areas, however, lunch is the main meal of the day. After this large lunch, schools and businesses close, and people stay home for an afternoon rest like the Spanish and Mexican *siesta*. Even during these quiet hours after lunch, the Greeks love to snack, and they munch on cookies and other sweets with their coffee.

Skewered Lamb/ Arní Souvlákia

Souvlákia *is especially good when cooked the Greek way—on an outdoor grill—but is also delicious when broiled in the oven. You can vary this* souvlákia *recipe by alternating pieces of marinated meat with chunks of green pepper, onion, and tomato. Leg of lamb is best for* souvlákia, *but you can also use beef or chicken. Inexpensive metal skewers are available at most grocery stores.*

2 tablespoons olive oil
3 tablespoons lemon juice
½ teaspoon salt
⅛ teaspoon pepper
½ teaspoon marjoram
2 pounds lamb, cut into 2-inch cubes
1 lemon, cut into wedges

1. Mix all ingredients except lamb and lemons in a large, flat dish.
2. Add lamb and stir to coat pieces well. Cover the dish with plastic wrap and let stand in refrigerator for at least 30 minutes.
3. Spear the cubes of meat onto 4 long metal skewers. Place skewers in a shallow broiling pan.
4. Place oven rack about 6 inches from top heat source. Turn on oven to broil.
5. Broil meat for 10 minutes. Then turn over the skewers and broil 10 minutes more.
6. Remove lamb from the skewers with a fork and serve with lemon wedges.

Serves 4

Souvlákia is often served atop a bed of white rice.

A flaky, buttery crust surrounds a filling of spinach, feta, scallions, and dill to make *spanikópita* a delicious treat for lunch, dinner, or snacktime.

Spinach Pie/
Spanikópita

Spanikópita, *or spinach pie, is one of the most famous Greek dishes. It is made with phyllo (FEE-low) pastry, which is tissue-thin dough sold either fresh or frozen. See page 22 for tips on handling this delicate dough.* Spanikópita *can be served hot as a main dish or side dish or cold as a snack or appetizer.*

2 **pounds fresh spinach (or 2 10-ounce packages frozen chopped spinach, thawed)**
¼ **cup olive oil**
½ **cup chopped scallions**
¼ **cup finely chopped fresh parsley**
2 **tablespoons finely chopped fresh dill, or 1 tablespoon dried dill weed**
4 **eggs, lightly beaten**
1 **cup (about 6 ounces) finely crumbled feta cheese**
½ **teaspoon salt**
¼ **teaspoon pepper**

dash of nutmeg
¾ cup (1½ sticks) butter or margarine, melted
½ pound (about 14 sheets) phyllo pastry, thawed

1. Preheat oven to 350°.
2. Remove large, tough stems from spinach leaves. Wash each spinach leaf in cold water to remove all dirt and sand. Using your hands, squeeze water from spinach and dry on paper towels.
3. Chop spinach into ¼-inch pieces. (If using frozen spinach, place thawed spinach in a colander and squeeze out excess moisture by pressing on spinach with the back of a large spoon.)
4. Heat olive oil in a large frying pan over medium-high heat. Add scallions and cook 4 minutes, stirring constantly. Add spinach and cook 3 more minutes.
5. Remove pan from heat and let cool for 5 minutes.
6. Stir in parsley, dill, eggs, feta cheese, salt, pepper, and nutmeg and set aside.
7. Butter a 9- by 13-inch baking pan. Place 1 sheet of phyllo pastry in pan. Brush sheet well with melted butter, then put another sheet on top of it. Continue adding sheets, brushing each one with butter, until there are a total of 7 sheets.
8. Spread spinach filling evenly over phyllo. Trim off dried edges with scissors or a sharp knife. Then fold excess phyllo over the filling.
9. Place 7 sheets of phyllo pastry over the spinach, one at a time, brushing each sheet well with melted butter before adding the next.
10. Trim off excess phyllo with a pair of scissors or a sharp knife. Brush top of pie with melted butter.
11. Place pan on middle oven rack and bake 40 minutes or until crust is golden.
12. Cool 5 minutes before cutting into squares.

Serves 8 to 12

WORKING WITH PHYLLO

Phyllo (FEE-low) dough is paper-thin dough made of flour and water that is used with various fillings for many Greek dishes. Phyllo dough is available frozen in many supermarkets and in specialty stores. Each sheet is brushed well with melted butter before baking. This makes the phyllo turn light, flaky, golden, and delicious.

Phyllo is extremely fragile, but using it is not difficult if you follow these basic rules:

1. Thaw frozen phyllo in its original package for 24 hours in the refrigerator.
2. Do not unwrap phyllo until you are ready to use it. Make sure your work area is cleared, your melted butter and pastry brush are ready, and your filling is prepared.
3. Remove rings from your fingers and make sure your fingernails are not too long. (Fingernails can tear the phyllo.)
4. Work with one sheet at a time. Peel sheets carefully from package.
5. After removing a sheet, cover remaining sheets tightly with either plastic wrap or a slightly damp kitchen towel (not terrycloth).
6. Leftover phyllo will stay fresh in the refrigerator for 1 week if covered well with plastic wrap.
7. If phyllo is not available where you live, you can substitute frozen puff pastry, thawed and rolled very thin with a rolling pin. It won't be as thin as phyllo, though, so use 1 or 2 fewer layers than called for in a recipe.

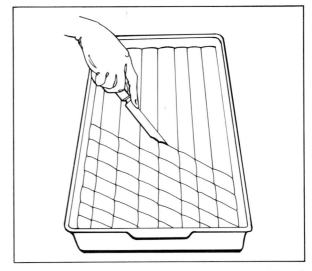

Dishes made with phyllo are often cut into traditional diamond shapes. Orange yogurt cake (p. 42) can also be served this way.

Greek Salad/
Saláta

Greeks always serve a salad with meals. The following recipe is the classic Greek salad featuring feta cheese.

½ **head iceberg or romaine lettuce**
2 **tomatoes, quartered, or 10 cherry tomatoes, cut in half**
1 **cucumber, peeled and sliced**
½ **green pepper, cored, seeded, and sliced**
5 **scallions, thinly sliced**
1 **cup (about 6 ounces) feta cheese, broken into chunks**
12 **to 16 black Greek olives**

1. Wash and prepare all vegetables.
2. Tear lettuce into bite-sized pieces and place in a large salad bowl.
3. Add tomatoes, cucumber, green pepper, scallions, feta cheese, and olives.
4. Pour dressing over salad and toss.
5. Serve on chilled salad plates.

Dressing:

2 **tablespoons red-wine vinegar**
1 **clove garlic, finely chopped**
¼ **teaspoon salt**
⅛ **teaspoon pepper**
½ **teaspoon oregano**
⅓ **cup olive oil**

1. Whisk together all ingredients except olive oil.
2. Slowly add the olive oil, whisking constantly.

Serves 4

APPETIZERS/
Mezéthes

In the late afternoon, many Greek people ward off their pre-dinner hunger by stopping by a cafe for refreshments. At Greek *tavernas,* adults sit and chat with friends while sipping on local wines and nibbling on *mezéthes,* or appetizers. These include olives, chunks of feta cheese, raw vegetables, bread, and dips. These *mezéthes,* plus soups, are also often served as the first course of a large meal.

Cucumber and Yogurt Dip/Tzatzíki

Cucumbers were brought to Greece from Asia centuries ago, and yogurt's origins are in the Middle East. The Greeks combine them in this refreshing méze, which is especially good on a hot day.

1 **medium cucumber**
1 **clove garlic, finely chopped**
3 **scallions, finely chopped**
1 **teaspoon olive oil**
½ **teaspoon white vinegar**
1 **teaspoon finely chopped fresh dill**
    or ½ teaspoon dried dill weed
1 **cup (8 ounces) plain, lowfat yogurt**

1. Peel cucumber. Cut in half lengthwise and scoop out and discard seeds. Cut into small chunks to make about 1 cup.
2. In a small bowl, mix cucumber with garlic, scallions, olive oil, vinegar, and dill.
3. Add yogurt and stir gently to combine.
4. Cover and chill 2 hours or more.
5. Serve salad-style on lettuce leaves garnished with tomato slices or as a dip with bread and raw vegetables.

Makes about 1¹/₂ cups

Eggplant Salad/
Melitzánosaláta

This méze *is called a salad, but it can also be served as a dip.*

1 1½- to 2-pound eggplant
1 clove garlic, finely chopped
2 tablespoons grated onion
¼ teaspoon salt
3 tablespoons olive oil
1 tablespoon lemon juice

1. Preheat oven to 350°.
2. Pierce the skin of the eggplant several times with a fork or with the tip of a sharp knife. Place eggplant on a cookie sheet and bake about 1 hour or until very soft.
3. Allow eggplant to cool well, then peel.
4. Chop the eggplant flesh or mash with a fork and place in a mixing bowl.
5. Add remaining ingredients and mix well. Cover and chill 2 to 3 hours before serving.

Makes about 2 cups

Prepare a Greek *mezéthes* platter of fresh vegetables and olives and serve with bread, *tzatziki (left)*, and *melitzánosalata*.

Stuffed Grape Leaves/ Dolmádes

Stuffed grape leaves are one of Greece's most famous—and most ancient—foods. Grape leaves can be purchased in jars at many supermarkets and specialty stores. They are packed in brine, or salt water, and must be rinsed thoroughly before using. You may want to ask a friend to help you fill and roll up the grape leaves.

2 **cups cooked white rice**
1 **pound ground lamb or ground beef**
½ **cup finely chopped scallions**
¼ **cup currants**
¼ **cup pine nuts or chopped almonds**
½ **teaspoon salt**
2 **tablespoons finely chopped fresh parsley**
2 **tablespoons olive oil**
1 **1-pound jar grape leaves**
¼ **cup lemon juice**
1 **10½-ounce can beef broth**
1 **cup water**
3 **lemons, cut into wedges**

1. Cook rice according to directions on package.
2. Place lamb or beef in a large skillet. Cook meat over medium-high heat until brown, stirring to break up into small pieces.
3. Remove meat from heat. Drain off fat and set aside.
4. In a large bowl, combine meat, rice, scallions, currants, nuts, salt, parsley, and olive oil. Stir gently with a spoon.
5. Drain grape leaves in a colander. Carefully rinse the grape leaves in cool running water. Drain on paper towels. Cut stem off leaves with a sharp knife.
6. Place 1 teaspoon meat mixture on a grape leaf and fold as shown. Repeat until all filling is used.
7. In a large saucepan, arrange the rolls in layers, seam-side down. Sprinkle 1 tablespoon of lemon juice over each layer.
8. Pour any remaining lemon juice, the beef broth, and the water over the *dolmádes*.

9. Place a heavy plate or baking dish on top of *dolmádes* to hold them in place while cooking. Cover saucepan and cook over low heat for 1 hour.

10. Remove from heat and allow to cool. Carefully remove the plate and drain off all cooking liquid.

11. Serve cold or at room temperature with lemon wedges.

Makes about 40 to 50 dolmádes

HOW TO STUFF A GRAPE LEAF

1. Place a grape leaf shiny side down on a plate or counter top, making sure leaf is flat.

2. Place 1 teaspoon of filling in the center of the leaf.

3. Fold stem end over filling.

4. Fold each side of leaf, one at a time, over filling, enclosing filling completely.

5. Roll up leaf from stem end toward the tip until you have a small, compact roll. Gently squeeze roll in the palm of your hand to seal edges.

6. Use rice fillings sparingly, and do not wrap grape leaves too tightly, as rice will expand.

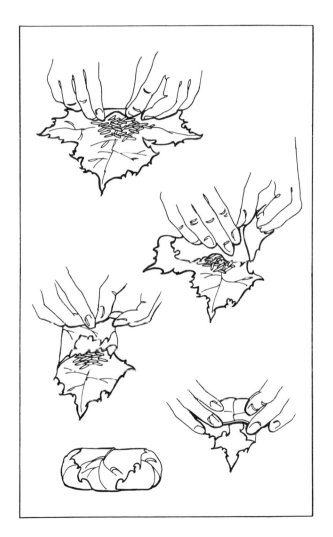

Stuffed with a filling of ground meat, rice, currants, and pine nuts, *dolmádes* are one of Greece's most ancient and best-loved foods. (Recipe on page 26.)

Lentil Soup/
Fakí

In Greece, fakí *is traditionally eaten on Good Friday. The Greek Orthodox Church prohibits eating meat or fish on that day, and lentil soup is a nourishing alternative. You can serve lentil soup as an appetizer or as a main dish.*

1 1-pound bag lentils
3 tablespoons olive oil
1 medium onion, finely chopped
1 stalk celery, finely chopped
2 carrots, peeled and cut into ⅛-inch-
    thick slices
2 cloves garlic, finely chopped
1 bay leaf
¼ teaspoon pepper
1 teaspoon oregano
2 tablespoons tomato paste
8 cups cold water
1 teaspoon salt
½ cup red-wine vinegar
½ cup chopped fresh parsley

1. Spread lentils evenly on a cookie sheet. Pick out any small stones or other foreign objects. Place lentils in a colander and rinse thoroughly with cold water.
2. Heat oil in a large kettle over medium-high heat. Add onions, celery, and carrots and sauté for 5 minutes.
3. Add lentils, garlic, bay leaf, pepper, oregano, tomato paste, and 8 cups cold water or enough to cover. Bring to a boil.
4. Cover kettle and simmer over low heat for 1 hour. (You may need to add more water if soup becomes too thick.)
5. Add salt and vinegar to lentil mixture and stir well. Cover and simmer, stirring occasionally, for 30 minutes more or until lentils are tender.
6. Stir in parsley and serve in individual soup bowls.

Serves 6 to 8

Fresh green parsley decorates delicate *soúpa avgolémono (left)* **and hearty** *fakí,* **two popular Greek soups.**

Egg and Lemon Soup/
Soúpa Avgolémono

Delicate egg and lemon soup is probably the number-one soup in Greece. Be careful to add the hot broth slowly to the eggs, beating all the while. The extra effort will be well worth it!

3 10½-ounce cans (about 4 cups) chicken broth
⅓ cup rice, uncooked
2 eggs
4 tablespoons lemon juice
4 thin slices lemon for garnish
2 teaspoons chopped fresh parsley for garnish

1. In a heavy saucepan, bring chicken broth to a boil. Turn down heat. Add rice and stir.
2. Cover pan and simmer 12 to 15 minutes or until rice is tender.
3. While rice is cooking, beat eggs and lemon juice together with a wire whisk. Set aside.
4. When rice is cooked, remove pan from heat.
5. Carefully add 2 cups hot broth to the egg-lemon mixture, a little at a time, whisking constantly. (If you add the broth too quickly or don't keep whisking, the eggs will curdle.)
6. Add the egg mixture to the remaining broth and rice and whisk together. Carefully reheat the soup, but *do not boil*.
7. Serve in soup bowls with a thin slice of lemon and a sprinkle of chopped fresh parsley floating on top.

Serves 4

DINNER/
Déipnon

In Greece, as in many other European countries, dinner is eaten rather late—often not until 10 P.M. At this time, the family comes together for an appetizer, salad, a meat or fish dish, vegetables, and potatoes, rice, or pasta. In the country, where lunch is the main meal of the day, people eat a smaller dinner, perhaps only a salad, cheese, and bread. Whether you serve the following Greek specialties at noon or in the evening, they are sure to please anyone's appetite.

Roast Chicken/
Kótapoulo Foúrnou

Lemon, garlic, and oregano are flavorings used widely in Greek cooking. This wonderfully fragrant combination of flavors penetrates the chicken as it roasts, and the result is delicious, moist, and very Greek. Keep the basting butter in a small saucepan on top of the stove where you can warm it as needed.

1 **3- to 3½-pound roasting chicken**
1 **tablespoon oregano**
2 **cloves garlic**
1 **lemon, cut in half**
½ **cup (1 stick) butter or margarine, melted**

1. Preheat oven to 350°.
2. Rinse chicken inside and out under cold running water and pat dry with paper towels.
3. Pour oregano into the chicken. Then place garlic and lemon halves inside.
4. Place chicken in a roasting pan. Roast uncovered 1½ to 1¾ hours, basting every 15 minutes with the melted butter.
5. Remove chicken from pan. Let chicken rest 10 minutes on serving platter before cutting.

Serves 4

Garnish Greek roast chicken with lemon wedges and serve orzo with browned butter sauce *(p. 36)* as a side dish.

Baked Fish/
Psári Plakí

Since Greece is surrounded by the sea, the Greeks eat many delicious fish and seafood dishes. For psári plakí*, cod, haddock, or bluefish fillets work well. If you use frozen fish fillets, thaw them completely before preparing this dish.*

2 tablespoons olive oil
2 pounds fish fillets
½ teaspoon salt
¼ teaspoon pepper
2 tablespoons lemon juice
1 medium onion, thinly sliced
¼ cup finely chopped fresh parsley
1 8-ounce can whole tomatoes

1. Preheat oven to 350°.
2. Brush a 9- by 13-inch baking dish with olive oil. Place fish in baking dish. Sprinkle with salt, pepper, and lemon juice.
3. Place onion slices on top of fish and sprinkle parsley over onion.
4. Drain tomatoes and break them into pieces with a spoon. Scatter tomato pieces over parsley.
5. Place on middle oven rack and bake 30 minutes or until tender, basting occasionally with pan juices.

Serves 4

Beef and Onion Stew/
Stifádo

Stifádo is a hearty stew that is especially good in cool weather. To vary this savory dish, add 1 cup of finely crumbled feta cheese before serving.

3 tablespoons vegetable oil
2 pounds beef chuck or top round,
       cut into 2-inch cubes
3 cups thinly sliced onions
2 cloves garlic, finely chopped
1 6-ounce can tomato paste
1 10½-ounce can beef broth
1 cup water
¼ cup red-wine vinegar
½ teaspoon salt

⅛ **teaspoon pepper**
¼ **teaspoon cinnamon**
1 bay leaf

1. In a dutch oven, heat oil over medium-high heat until it begins to sizzle.
2. Add meat and brown on all sides. When browned, remove meat with a spatula or a slotted spoon and set aside.
3. Put onions and garlic in the dutch oven and cook until lightly browned.
4. Return meat to the dutch oven. Add tomato paste, beef broth, water, wine vinegar, and seasonings, and mix well.
5. Cover dutch oven and turn heat to low. Simmer stew about 3 to 4 hours or until the meat is very tender. Stir every 15 minutes to prevent meat from sticking to the dutch oven. The sauce will become very thick, almost like jam.
6. Remove bay leaf and serve.

Serves 4 to 6

As *stifádo* simmers, the onions become sweet, the sauce thick and flavorful, and the meat tender.

Orzo with Browned Butter Sauce/ Órzo Kaúto Voútyro

Orzo is a rice-shaped pasta available at most supermarkets. If you can't get orzo, you can substitute any small pasta or white rice.

½ **pound orzo, uncooked**
⅓ **cup butter or margarine**
3 **tablespoons grated Parmesan cheese**

1. Cook pasta according to directions on package. Drain in a colander and set aside.
2. While pasta is cooking, put butter in a small saucepan. Melt over medium-high heat and cook until butter turns brown.
3. Place hot, drained pasta in a serving bowl. Pour butter and Parmesan cheese over pasta and stir to combine. Serve immediately.

Serves 4

Baked Potatoes Oregano/ Patátes Foúrno Riganátes

4 **large potatoes**
3 **tablespoons olive oil**
1½ **tablespoons lemon juice**
½ **teaspoon oregano**
½ **teaspoon salt**

1. Scrub potatoes under cool running water. Place in a large, heavy saucepan with enough water to cover potatoes completely.
2. Boil potatoes over medium-high heat 20 to 25 minutes or until fairly soft but not mushy. Drain in a colander and cool to room temperature, then peel.
3. Preheat oven to 350°.
4. Slice potatoes into ¼-inch-thick slices and place in a 1-quart baking dish.
5. Pour olive oil over potatoes. Then add lemon juice, oregano, and salt. Stir *very gently* to prevent potato slices from breaking.
6. Bake uncovered for 20 minutes.

Serves 4

Rice Pilaf/
Piláfi

Sautéing the rice before boiling cooks the starch on the outside of each grain and keeps it from sticking together.

3 tablespoons butter or margarine
2 cups long-grain rice, uncooked
5 cups water or 4 10½-ounce cans
    chicken broth
1 teaspoon salt

1. Melt butter in heavy saucepan over medium-high heat.
2. Add rice and sauté, stirring constantly, about 5 minutes or until rice is transparent.
3. Add water or broth and salt. Bring to a boil.
4. Cover pan, turn heat to lowest setting, and simmer 15 to 20 minutes or until liquid is absorbed and rice is tender.

Serves 4 to 6

Fried Zucchini/
Kolokithákia Tiganíta

4 small zucchini
½ cup all-purpose flour
¼ teaspoon salt
    dash of pepper
½ cup olive oil

1. Scrub zucchini and cut into ¼-inch-thick slices.
2. In a clean brown paper bag, combine flour, salt, and pepper.
3. Put zucchini slices in the bag and shake gently to coat all slices.
4. In a large, heavy frying pan, heat oil over medium-high heat.
5. Fry zucchini slices, one layer at a time, until golden brown.
6. Carefully turn zucchini with a spatula and brown other side.
7. Remove cooked zucchini with spatula or slotted spoon and drain on paper towels.

Serves 4

The wonderful fresh vegetables grown in Greece are served in many different ways. Fried zucchini *(left)* and stuffed tomatoes with feta are two Greek favorites.

Stuffed Tomatoes with Feta Cheese/ Domátes mé Féta

For this recipe, it is important to use the reddest, ripest tomatoes available. If your tomatoes aren't quite ripe (pinkish-orange instead of bright red), place them in a brown paper bag and keep in a cupboard or other dark place for a day or two to ripen.

4 ripe, medium tomatoes
2 tablespoons finely chopped scallions
2 tablespoons finely chopped fresh parsley
½ cup (about 3 ounces) finely crumbled feta cheese
¼ cup bread crumbs
3 tablespoons olive oil

1. Carefully cut tops off tomatoes. Using a spoon, carefully scoop out pulp and seeds. Save pulp and discard seeds.

2. Coarsely chop the tomato pulp.
3. Preheat oven to 350°.
4. In a small bowl, combine tomato pulp with scallions, parsley, feta cheese, bread crumbs, and olive oil.
5. Spoon mixture into the hollowed-out tomatoes. Place tomatoes right side up in an 8- by 8-inch baking pan and bake 15 minutes.
6. Serve stuffed tomatoes steaming hot.

Serves 4

DESSERT/
Disert

Although most Greeks end their meals with a simple dessert of cold fresh fruit, you may want to top off your Greek feasts with one of the following recipes. The Greek people love sweets of all kinds, and you and your family will enjoy these Greek treats, too.

Butter Cookies/
Kourabiéthes

Butter cookies are very popular year-round in Greece. At Christmastime, they are topped with whole cloves to symbolize the spices brought by the Wise Men.

2½ cups all-purpose flour
1 teaspoon baking powder
¼ teaspoon salt
1 cup (2 sticks) butter, softened
½ cup sugar
1 egg
½ teaspoon vanilla extract
¼ teaspoon almond extract
powdered sugar for sprinkling

1. Preheat oven to 350°.
2. In a small bowl, combine flour, baking powder, and salt.
3. In a large bowl, beat together butter, sugar, and egg until light and fluffy. Add flour mixture to butter mixture and mix until well blended. Add vanilla and almond extracts and mix well.
4. With your hands, form dough, about ½ tablespoon at a time, into balls, crescents, or S-shapes.
5. Place cookies 2 inches apart on cookie sheet. Put on middle oven rack and bake 15 to 18 minutes or until barely brown around the edges.
7. Remove from cookie sheet with spatula and cool on wire rack for 5 minutes.
8. With a flour sifter, sift powdered sugar over cookies.

Makes about 3 dozen cookies

Fruit and Yogurt/
Fróuta ké Yaoúrtí

1 cup (8 ounces) plain, lowfat yogurt
3 tablespoons honey
1½ tablespoons grated lemon rind
4 cups cut-up mixed fresh fruit (such as grapes, melon, orange segments, peaches, and berries)
¼ cup slivered almonds

1. In a medium mixing bowl, combine yogurt, honey, and lemon rind.
2. Put fruit and almonds in serving bowl. Stir gently to combine.
3. Pour yogurt mixture over fruit and serve in individual dessert bowls.

Serves 4 to 6

Serve *fróuta ké yaoúrti* with buttery *kourabiéthes* for a refreshing dessert.

Orange Yogurt Cake/ Toúrta mé Portokáli ké Yaoúrtí

Cake:

2½ cups all-purpose flour
2 teaspoons baking powder
1 teaspoon baking soda
½ teaspoon salt
1 teaspoon cinnamon
3 eggs
1 cup sugar
¾ cup (1½ sticks) butter or margarine, melted
2 teaspoons grated orange peel
1 teaspoon vanilla extract
1 cup (8 ounces) plain, lowfat yogurt
½ cup orange juice
1 cup (¼ pound) finely ground walnuts

1. Preheat oven to 350°.
2. Butter a 9- by 13-inch cake pan and lightly flour the bottom and sides of pan.
3. In a medium bowl, combine flour, baking powder, baking soda, salt, and cinnamon.

4. In a large mixing bowl, beat together eggs and sugar until light and foamy. Add melted butter, orange peel, and vanilla extract and mix well.
5. Add yogurt, orange juice, and combined dry ingredients to egg mixture, a little at a time, beating well after each addition. Fold in walnuts.
6. Pour batter into baking pan and smooth the top. Place on middle oven rack and bake for 45 minutes or until cake pulls away from sides of pan and a toothpick inserted in the center comes out clean. While cake is baking, make the syrup.

Syrup:

1 cup sugar
½ cup water
½ cup orange juice
1 stick cinnamon
2 pieces orange peel (about 1 inch by 2 inches each)

1. Combine all syrup ingredients in a small saucepan.

2. Bring sauce to a boil over high heat. Lower heat and simmer for 10 minutes.

3. Remove pan from heat and cool. When cool, remove the cinnamon stick and orange peel.

4. Pour syrup over cake while cake is still warm.

5. When cake is cool, cut into diamonds or squares and serve on dessert plates.

Serves 8 to 12

Rice Pudding/ Rizógalo

Rice pudding is a popular dessert in Greece. It is also eaten for breakfast.

⅓ **cup white rice, uncooked**
4 **cups (1 quart) milk**
½ **cup sugar**
¼ **cup (½ stick) butter or margarine**
½ **teaspoon salt**
4 **eggs, lightly beaten**
   grated rind of 1 orange
1 **teaspoon vanilla extract**
   cinnamon for sprinkling

1. In a heavy saucepan, combine rice, milk, sugar, butter, and salt.

2. Simmer uncovered over medium heat for 45 minutes or until very thick and creamy. Stir frequently to prevent scorching.

3. Remove pan from heat. Quickly beat in eggs, orange rind, and vanilla extract.

4. Return pan to low heat. Cook, stirring constantly, about 10 minutes or until thickened.

5. Pour rice pudding into serving dish and sprinkle with cinnamon.

6. Serve warm, at room temperature, or cold.

Serves 4 to 6

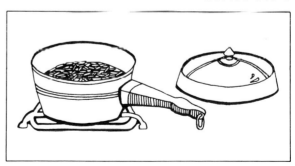

Simmer rice pudding slowly until it becomes thick and creamy.

Honey Cheese Pie/
Melópitta

4 eggs
2 cups (16 ounces) ricotta cheese
1 cup honey
½ teaspoon cinnamon
2 tablespoons all-purpose flour
1 teaspoon lemon juice
  cinnamon for sprinkling

1. Preheat oven to 350°.
2. Beat eggs lightly in a large mixing bowl.
3. Add ricotta cheese, honey, cinnamon, flour, and lemon juice. Beat for 3 minutes or until very smooth.
4. Rub 1 tablespoon butter in a 9-inch pie pan, then pour in pie mixture.
5. Place on middle oven rack and bake 1 hour or until the surface of the pie cracks and is puffed.
6. Remove from oven and sprinkle with cinnamon.
7. Cool to room temperature before cutting into wedges to serve.

Serves 8 to 10

Walnut-Honey Pastry/
Baklavá

Baklavá *is no doubt the favorite and best-known Greek dessert. This sweet pastry is made with phyllo dough, so read over the instructions on page 22 for tips on working with the fragile phyllo sheets.*

Syrup:

1 cup sugar
1 cup water
1 ½-inch-thick slice lemon
1 stick cinnamon
1 cup honey

1. In a small saucepan, combine sugar, water, lemon slice, and cinnamon stick.
2. Bring to a boil over medium heat. Reduce heat and simmer 10 minutes.
3. Remove pan from heat. Stir in honey and cool well.
4. When cool, remove the lemon slice and cinnamon stick.

Pastry:

4 cups (1 pound) finely ground walnuts
2 cups (½ pound) finely ground blanched or unblanched almonds
¼ cup sugar
2 teaspoons cinnamon
½ teaspoon nutmeg
1½ cups (3 sticks) butter or margarine, melted
1 1-pound package phyllo pastry, thawed

1. Preheat oven to 300°.
2. In a large bowl, combine walnuts, almonds, sugar, cinnamon, and nutmeg.
3. Butter a 9- by 13-inch pan with 2 tablespoons butter.
4. Place 4 sheets of phyllo in the pan, brushing each with melted butter before adding the next. Butter the fourth sheet also.
5. Sprinkle ½ to ¾ cup of nut mixture over the phyllo.
6. Top nut mixture with 2 more sheets of phyllo, buttering each sheet well.
7. Continue alternating nut mixture with 2 sheets buttered phyllo until both are used up, ending with phyllo. Brush top with butter.
8. With a sharp knife, trim off any excess phyllo on the sides of the pastry.
9. With a sharp knife, cut 1½-inch-wide lengthwise strips in the dough. (Do not cut all the way through the dough. Cut through the top layer only.)
10. Make 1½-inch diagonal cuts to create diamond-shaped pieces. (Again, cut through the top layer only.)
11. Bake for 1 hour or until golden brown.
12. Remove from oven and place on a cooling rack.
13. Cut through diamonds completely with a sharp knife. Immediately pour the cooled syrup over hot pastry.
14. Cool and serve on dessert plates.

Makes about 3 dozen pieces

Layer upon layer of flaky, buttery phyllo, nutmeg-spiced walnuts and almonds, and a sweet honey sauce make *baklavá* an unforgettable treat. (Recipe on page 44.)

THE CAREFUL COOK

Whenever you cook, there are certain safety rules you must always keep in mind. Even experienced cooks follow these rules when they are in the kitchen.

1. Always wash your hands before handling food.
2. Thoroughly wash all raw vegetables and fruits to remove dirt, chemicals, and insecticides.
3. Use a cutting board when cutting up vegetables and fruits. Don't cut them up in your hand! And be sure to cut in a direction *away* from you and your fingers.
4. Long hair or loose clothing can easily catch fire if brought near the burners of a stove. If you have long hair, tie it back before you start cooking.
5. Turn all pot handles toward the back of the stove so that you will not catch your sleeves or jewelry on them. This is especially important when younger brothers and sisters are around. They could easily knock off a pot and get burned.
6. Always use a pot holder to steady hot pots or to take pans out of the oven. Don't use a wet cloth on a hot pan because the steam it produces could burn you.
7. Lift the lid of a steaming pot with the opening away from you so that you will not get burned.
8. If you get burned, hold the burn under cold running water. Do not put grease or butter on it. Cold water helps to take the heat out, but grease or butter will only keep it in.
9. If grease or cooking oil catches fire, throw baking soda or salt at the bottom of the flame to put it out. (Water will *not* put out a grease fire.) Call for help, and try to turn all the stove burners to "off."

Skewered Lamb / **Arní Souvlákia** / ΑΡΝΙ ΣΟΥΒΛΑΚΙΑ
Spinach Pie / **Spanikópita** / ΣΠΑΝΑΚΟΠΗΤΑ
Greek Salad / **Saláta** / ΣΑΛΑΤΑ
Cucumber and Yogurt Dip / **Tzatzíki** / ΤΖΑΤΖΙΚΙ
Eggplant Salad / **Melitzánosaláta** / ΜΕΛΙΤΖΑΝΟΣΑΛΑΤΑ
Stuffed Grape Leaves / **Dolmádes** / ΝΤΟΛΜΑΔΕΣ
Lentil Soup / **Fakí** / ΦΑΚΗ
Egg and Lemon Soup / **Soúpa Avgolémono** / ΣΟΥΠΑ ΑΥΓΟΛΕΜΟΝΟ
Roast Chicken / **Kótapoulo Foúrnou** / ΚΟΤΑ ΦΟΥΡΝΟΥ
Baked Fish / **Psári Plakí** / ΨΑΡΙ ΠΛΑΚΙ
Beef and Onion Stew / **Stifádo** / ΣΤΙΦΑΔΟ
Orzo with Browned Butter Sauce / **Órzo Kaúto Voútyro** / ΟΡΖΟ ΚΑΥΤΟ ΒΟΥΤΥΡΟ
Baked Potatoes Oregano / **Patátes Foúrno Riganátes** / ΠΑΤΑΤΕΣ ΦΟΥΡΝΟ ΡΥΓΑΝΑΤΕΣ
Rice Pilaf / **Piláfi** / ΠΙΛΑΦΙ
Fried Zucchini / **Kolokithákia Tiganíta** / ΚΟΛΟΚΥΘΑΚΙΑ ΤΗΓΑΝΙΤΑ
Stuffed Tomatoes with Feta Cheese / **Domátes mé Féta** / ΝΤΟΜΑΤΕΣ ΜΕ ΦΕΤΑ
Butter Cookies / **Kourabiéthes** / ΚΟΥΡΑΜΠΙΕΔΕΣ
Fruit and Yogurt / **Fróuta ké Yaoúrtí** / ΦΡΟΥΤΑ ΚΑΙ ΓΙΑΟΥΡΤΙ
Orange Yogurt Cake / **Toúrta mé Portokáli ké Yaoúrtí** / ΤΟΥΡΤΑ ΜΕ ΠΟΡΤΟΚΑΛΙ ΚΑΙ ΓΙΑΟΥΡΤΙ
Rice Pudding / **Rizógalo** / ΡΙΖΟΓΑΛΟ
Honey Cheese Pie / **Melópitta** / ΜΕΛΟΠΙΤΤΑ
Walnut-Honey Pastry / **Baklavá** / ΜΠΑΚΛΑΒΑΣ

Breakfast / **Próyefma** / ΠΡΟΓΕΥΜΑ
Lunch / **Yéfma** / ΓΕΥΜΑ
Appetizers / **Mezéthes** / ΜΕΖΕΔΕΣ
Dinner / **Déipnon** / ΔΕΙΠΝΟ
Dessert / **Disert** / ΔΗΖΕΡΤ

METRIC CONVERSION CHART

WHEN YOU KNOW		MULTIPLY BY	TO FIND	
MASS (weight)				
ounces	(oz)	28.0	grams	(g)
pounds	(lb)	0.45	kilograms	(kg)
VOLUME				
teaspoons	(tsp)	5.0	milliliters	(ml)
tablespoons	(Tbsp)	15.0	milliliters	
fluid ounces	(oz)	30.0	milliliters	
cup	(c)	0.24	liters	(l)
pint	(pt)	0.47	liters	
quart	(qt)	0.95	liters	
gallon	(gal)	3.8	liters	
TEMPERATURE				
Fahrenheit	(°F)	5/9 (after	Celsius	(°C)
temperature		subtracting 32)	temperature	

COMMON MEASURES AND THEIR EQUIVALENTS

3 teaspoons = 1 tablespoon

8 tablespoons = ½ cup

2 cups = 1 pint

2 pints = 1 quart

4 quarts = 1 gallon

16 ounces = 1 pound

INDEX

(recipes indicated by **bold face** *type)*

ABOUT THE AUTHOR

Lynne W. Villios, a native of St. Charles, Minnesota, graduated from St. Olaf College in Northfield, Minnesota, with a degree in political science. Later she graduated from Vanderbilt University Law School in Tennessee. She currently lives in New York City and is an investment banker working with state and local governments.

Villios learned Greek cooking from her husband's relatives. His grandparents came to the United States from Macedonia before World War I and settled in New York. Today, Villios enjoys authentic Greek specialties made by her husband's aunts, and she often visits New York's many fine Greek restaurants. Villios is an accomplished cook and often makes Greek meals for her friends and family. In addition to cooking, Villios enjoys reading, traveling, and collecting antiques.

Pśari plakí is just one of many delicious Greek fish specialties. (Recipe on page 34.)

DATE DUE

JUN 1 '99			
MAR 0 5 '01			
APR 0 9 '09			
		DISCARD	